HEALING AND THE AUTHORITY OF THE BELIEVER

HEALING AND THE AUTHORITY OF THE BELIEVER

DR. CHÉ AHN

Wagner Publications

Healing and the Authority of the Believer
Copyright © 1999
by Ché Ahn
Second Printing: October, 1999
ISBN 1-58502-003-6

Published by
Wagner Publications
11005 N. Highway 83, Suite 119
Colorado Springs, CO 80921

Rights for publishing this book in other languages are contracted by Gospel Literature International (GLINT). GLINT also provides technical help for the adaptation, translation, and publishing of Bible study resources and books in scores of languages worldwide. For further information, contact GLINT, P.O. Box 4060, Ontario, CA 91761-1003, USA, Email: glintint@aol.com, or the publisher.

TABLE OF CONTENTS

AN HOUR FOR HEALING

We are living in an incredible "kairos" or appointed hour when God is raising up saints with greater spiritual authority. Perhaps unlike any other previous time, God is raising up believers everywhere to carry the healing anointing in fullness and the authority of Jesus Christ to see incredible miracles. He is not just imparting this gifting and faith to a few – but I believe He wants to impart to humble, obedient, "nameless" and "faceless" Christians everywhere.

As we stand on the verge of revival, in a time when multitudes are in distress, God stands out as the only source of true hope and help for this generation. He is asking us to believe Him at His Word and become instruments of His authority to demonstrate His reality. He is asking us to walk in miracles and give them away – miracles to see the dead raised, AIDS patients healed, blind eyes opened, deaf ears unstopped, and the advancement of His kingdom by the visible evidence of His hand. He wants to give us greater spiritual authority in our lives that we might be about His business and glorify His name.

This small book is simply an instrument to fuel your faith and unveil your eyes and heart to the marvelous calling and provision God has already made for you. May He come and abide with you, equip you, teach you, and impart to you your portion in this vital hour. In Jesus' glorious name!

———◆———

IMPARTATION AND ACTIVATION OF SPIRITUAL AUTHORITY

A new measure of healing authority came into my life and ministry in 1994. I had been a Christian and a pastor for many years and had seen God do many extraordinary things. I used to be in charge of the weekly healing room for a youth movement that had more than 2,000 in attendance, and I remember one evening when 20 people in the room all had their vision problems healed. Far sighted, near sighted, and needing contacts or glasses – all were healed that night. It was one of the most amazing and sovereign acts of God's healing power that I had ever witnessed.

Yet the incidence of healings throughout my 15-plus years of ministry were dotted between long dry spells. In fact, in the '80s, healings were rare and most people got worse when I prayed for them. I have often said that "the '80s were from Hades." It was hard doing ministry during that season of my life.

In 1994, things changed. I was invited to attend a healing

conference at the Anaheim Vineyard with Mahesh Chavda and Francis McNutt. Both men are well known for vital and powerful healing ministries.

This conference in itself was a wonder to me (I share the detailed account in my book *Into The Fire*, Renew Books). It was my first exposure to "renewal," or the manifest presence of God, that began to be poured out that year in both Anaheim, California, and Toronto, Canada. Renewal is marked by unusual "manifestations" of the presence of the Holy Spirit on people such as laughing, shaking, jerking, or falling under the power of the Holy Spirit. Generally, there is also a charged atmosphere filled with a kind of "liquid love" of the Lord and revelation of His true nature.

All of this was new to me. I searched as a hungry man, wanting all God had for me at the conference, though not yet understanding the impact of His generosity. What happened that week in regard to moving in a healing anointing and authority was astounding. It began with a dream told by Mahesh Chavda as he was preaching on healing.

Two Loaves of Bread Changed My Life

The night before his session, Mahesh had a dream about a pastor who brought two loaves of bread to the conference. He said he believed it was a symbolic dream, and that the pastor represented all of the pastors who were in attendance (I'd estimate that there were between 500-700 pastors at the conference of 4,000). Mahesh explained that he believed the bread represented the healing anointing. He alluded to the Scripture where the Syrophoenician woman came to Jesus and asked Him to please come and heal her daughter. Jesus replied that it was not good to "give the children's bread to the dogs." Mahesh believed the bread to be the healing anointing. The woman, barred by the Law from directly accessing that blessing, replied that "even the dogs could eat the crumbs from the children's table." Her faith was great, and she was given the miracle she needed for her daughter.

As Mahesh summarized his dream in relation to this passage, he spoke a release and an injunctive to us as pastors. He told us to take the anointing, represented by the two loaves, or double portion of bread he had seen, back to our local churches and minister the healing anointing to our people. As he was issuing this wonderful mandate, I could hardly contain myself. It was all I could do to stay in my seat. I wanted to stand up and shout, wave at Mahesh, and get his attention – even though he didn't know me from Adam.

You see, right before I left for the conference, my wife gave me two loaves of bread that I had brought with me! I had never brought bread to any conference before, nor have I since. I had merely given my wife a bread maker during the Christmas season, and she had been experimenting by baking bread every day. As I walked out the door to leave for Anaheim, she handed me two loaves of raisin bread and suggested that I munch on them whenever I was hungry.

I thanked her and didn't think too much about it until Mahesh shared his dream. When he specified he saw a pastor with two loaves of bread, I said to myself, "That's me! That's not some general word of knowledge, I mean, that's me, and I claim that promise as my own!"

A PRAYER FOR IMPARTATION AND ACTIVATION

I didn't want to make a scene, so I waited until after the service had finished to approach Mahesh. I stood patiently in line with many others as he was praying for people. When he finally got to me, I said, "Mahesh, you don't know me (since then we've become very good friends), but I am a pastor and I literally brought two loaves of bread to this conference." I explained how my wife handed me the two loaves. Mahesh seemed intent, and told me to wait right where I was standing. He rushed back to the platform and grabbed the microphone. At that moment, he said, "Ladies and gentlemen," and everyone stopped doing what he or she was doing. He continued, "There's a pastor here who brought two loaves of bread to the conference, just like in my dream. I want us to pray for him now."

Instantly I felt as though a thousand eyeballs were piercing the back of my head. I wasn't expecting this at all. As he laid his hands on me to pray, I went flying backwards. There were no helpers or catchers – I literally flew to the floor and shook violently under an incredibly powerful anointing of the Holy Spirit. I was "out" under the Spirit's power, and didn't quite know what had happened to me. But I knew it was something significant.

There had been a powerful impartation when Mahesh prayed for me, though I didn't fully understand it at the time. It was a life changing conference, to say the least. Truthfully, I had no idea then of the historic timing of that conference or that it fell at the beginning of a new outpouring which we now know as the Renewal. Yet from that point on, everything changed for me. Looking back to what happened that January 1994, I believe more than an impartation of anointing was given to me. I believe that God activated my spiritual authority to take His healing anointing to the sick and hurting.

A Blind Girl Healed!

The next week I was doing a youth conference for *Rock the Nations* with about 250 kids. I was one of four or five main speakers and was doing a workshop. I don't even remember the topic on which I shared, but afterwards, a young girl about 14 years old came up to me. She had been waiting in line for prayer, and when it was her turn, she said, "Could you please pray for my left eye? I'm blind in my left eye." She explained that she was at a carnival when a metal object flew out of the air, hitting her directly in the pupil. She had undergone three eye surgeries but still could not see a thing. Her eye was completely dark. As she described the details of her blindness, I felt whatever ounce of faith I had begin to dissipate.

The reason is that I had never seen a blind person get healed. In all the years that I had prayed for people before (such as the healing room of that 2000 member Bible study in Washing-

---
♦

I AM MORE AND MORE CONVINCED THAT GOD
WANTS TO RELEASE A WHOLE ARMY
TO WALK IN A NEW DIMENSION OF HEALING
AND THE MIRACULOUS

♦
---

ton, D.C.), I had seen people come out of wheelchairs, deaf people hear, nearsighted vision get healed, but I had never seen a totally blind eye opened.

Yet, when you are a pastor, you pray. The young woman was asking for prayer, and I was willing. I asked her to place her hand over her eye, and I put my hand over her hand. I don't know what I prayed, but I will never forget the expression on her face. All of a sudden, she started to scream and cry, and she said, "I can see your eyes, I can see your face, I can see you!" And I said, "Really????" I was totally in unbelief. I couldn't believe it! All of a sudden, I flashed back to the Healing Conference the week before when Mahesh had prayed for me, and I thought, "Is it possible that something was activated and imparted to me and that's why something happened?"

An impartation and activation had taken place. A miracle was the result. I want to encourage you to be in faith that God wants to impart something to you and release greater spiritual authority in your life, even as you read the pages of this book. God can do something for you. Don't be passive about the great gifts and blessings of the Lord. Expect an impartation, receive an activation, and then use it for His glory!

WE NEED POWER *AND* AUTHORITY

Since that day, I am more and more convinced that God wants to release a whole army to walk in a new dimension of healing and the miraculous. Frankly, there are billions of people around the world who have never heard the gospel. In order for this to come to pass, I believe we need to see every single man, woman, and child possible anointed with the Holy Spirit to take the healing authority and truth to the nations in order for us to fulfill the Great Commission!

One of the greatest ways this will happen is if we not only embrace God's desire to give us this power in healing, but if we fully understand our authority as believers and walk in it. In fact, the authority God has given to us as believers in Jesus the Messiah, I believe, is one of the keys to fulfilling the Great Commission that has been overlooked by the body of Christ. When we talk about reaching the lost, we emphasize power and anointing, but tend to overlook spiritual authority. We need both the power *and* the authority to get the job done.

The best way to define power and authority is to describe or illustrate how power and authority work. A Mack truck is powerful, but a policewoman, who is not as "powerful" as the truck, can stop the truck right in the middle of traffic because she has authority to do so. God has given to us both power and authority, but this book is devoted to the subject of spiritual authority and healing. I would like to use James 5:13-18 as the primary text for this important subject:

"Is any one of you in trouble? He should pray. Is anyone happy? Let him sing songs of praise. Is any one of you sick? He should call the elders of the church to pray over him and anoint him with oil in the name of the Lord. And the prayer offered in faith will make the sick person well; the Lord will raise him up. If he has sinned, he will be forgiven. Therefore confess your sins to each other and pray for each other so that you may be healed. The prayer of a righteous man is powerful and effective. Elijah was a man just like us. He prayed earnestly that it would not rain, and it did not rain on the land for three and a half years. Again he prayed, and the heavens gave rain, and the earth produced its crops."

Although this text does not speak of or specifically mention spiritual authority, it is implied throughout these six verses. Although this text does speak clearly on the subject of healing, I would like to share principles of spiritual authority in reference to healing with you from this text in James. Let's begin.

---◆---

CHAPTER ONE

AUTHORITY OF BELIEVERS

In James 5:13, James states: "Is any one of you in trouble? He should pray." James is specifically writing to the Jewish believers who were scattered around the then known world. "James, a servant of God and of the Lord Jesus Christ, To the twelve tribes scattered among the nations: Greetings" (James 1:1). But this word applies to everyone who calls on the name of Jesus. If we are in trouble, God has given us the authority to come before His presence and to pray. Through prayer we can exercise incredible spiritual authority.

A BUSINESSMAN WITH SPIRITUAL AUTHORITY

Recently, Carlos Annacondia spoke at our church, Harvest Rock Church, here in Pasadena, California. He is an Argentine evangelist whom God has raised up. I have heard Dr. Peter Wagner say many times that in just ten years, Carlos has led more than one million people to the Lord. I believe

God has raised him up as a prophetic sign to this generation of what is to come. Carlos is not a pastor, he has not been to Bible College, and he has not been ordained. I believe that he has only a sixth grade education and has become a very successful businessman. But what sets Carlos apart is his tremendous spiritual authority and his ability to exercise that authority.

Annacondia has such an impact when he visits a city in Argentina that residents actually describe their cities as "before Annacondia" and "after Annacondia." Things happen when Annacondia comes. He moves in extraordinary healing, miracles, and corporate deliverance. He knows how to call upon and embrace the authority of Jesus in his ministry. Consider the title of his book, *Listen To Me, Satan* (Creation House), and you begin to envision the kind of authority that

---

AS BELIEVERS, GOD TELLS US
TO LAY OUR HANDS ON THE SICK AND THEY WILL
RECOVER. DO YOU BELIEVE
THAT *YOU* HAVE THAT AUTHORITY?

---

this man has. He shares one story in the book about a mother who brought a child suffering from Down's Syndrome to his service. The child had all of the unmistakable distinguishing characteristics and the mental handicaps associated with the disease. When the anointing came upon that child, his genetic make up completely changed instantaneously, and the child's face and body became normal right there on the spot (*Listen To Me Satan*, p. 33)!

As I began to study Carlos Annacondia, devour his reading materials, and sit under his ministry (I went to Argentina in 1991), a major truth began to hit me. In this current visitation of God, or Renewal, we talk about the power of the Holy Spirit –which we should. We talk about the anointing of the Holy Spirit, which is essential to move in power. We even talk about how to move in the healing anointing, and that's imperative. But we have yet to really emphasize the reality and purpose of spiritual authority.

AUTHORITY IN THE NEW TESTAMENT

Consider the miracles that were released in the New Testament. When Jesus sent His disciples out to heal the sick and cast out demons, He first gave them *authority* (see Matthew 10:1). It doesn't say He prayed to give them more anointing. It doesn't say He gave them a special healing anointing. It says He gave them *authority* over unclean spirits and to heal all kinds of sickness. We need authority to get the job done. The King James Version translates Matthew 10:1 as Jesus giving them "power." But the Greek word is *exousia,* which is better translated as authority.

Likewise, in Matthew 28, where Jesus issues the Great Commission, He delivers it with authority. I believe the Great Commission to "Go and make disciples of all nations" really begins with verse 18. In that verse, Jesus uses the same Greek word *exousia* when He says, "All *authority* has been given to Me in heaven and on earth...go therefore and make disciples..." (NKJ, italics added). This is the key to the Great Commission. Jesus is saying that we are going to be able to make disciples of all nations through *His* authority. By His authority and under His delegated authority, we will each have *authority*, and we will be able to take nations for Him!

We need authority to fulfill the Great Commission. We need authority to preach, drive out demons, and heal the sick.

In Mark's version of the Great Commission, Jesus says, "These signs *will* follow those who *believe*: In My name, they will cast out demons; they will speak with new tongues; they will take up serpents; and if they drink anything deadly, it will by no means hurt them; they will lay hands on the sick, and they will recover" (Mark 16:17, NKJ, italics added).

It does not say these signs will follow only the apostles or evangelists, or those who are well known. Rather, it says these signs will follow *all* that believe. Every believer who calls on the name of the Lord has that kind of authority, just as the passage in James 5 says if you are in trouble, pray. The word "trouble" here means trials and tribulation, and can also encompass sickness, demonic warfare, and oppression from the enemy. Thus the Lord is instructing us that when we, as believers, are in trouble, we should pray. He is saying He has given us authority as believers to address what comes our way.

AUTHORITY FOR EVERY BELIEVER

Again, God expresses His desire to raise up all peoples to do marvelous things in Joel 2 and Acts 2. He declares He will pour out His Spirit on all flesh, our sons and daughters will prophesy, our old men will dream dreams, our young men will see visions, and even upon His servants will He pour out His Spirit. At the time Joel was written, the people whom God chose to highlight were the nameless and faceless people, the hidden "average guy," and particularly those who were not respected in society.

Women were not respected, kids were not respected, and the elderly were not respected. Remember the story when the youths began to make fun of Elisha, calling him baldy (2 Kings 2:23-25)? That was not respect. Servants were especially considered a low class of society, not worthy of respect. Yet

God highlights these very groups of people and declares that these are the ones He wants to anoint and raise up in the last days. God simply wants to use every one of us! He is calling forth the *authority* of *every* believer!

When God says He has given *you* "authority to trample on snakes and scorpions and to overcome all the power of the enemy" (Luke 10:19), do you believe that? One of the things that I love most about this Renewal is that not just a few people are walking in this authority. The authority is being exercised by the masses. It is being given to all of us. We have kids in our church that serve on the ministry team. If you really want powerful ministry, have one of these children pray for you, and you will see the authority of God!

In Toronto, a girl with dyslexia was healed during the service and was able to read words clearly for the first time. God rewired her right there and then used her to heal others of dyslexia. It's kids! It's women! It's *everyone* God wants to use! It's you (*Catch the Fire*, pp. 170-172)!

Mark Dupont from Toronto shared a story with us when he came to speak at our church that absolutely amazed me. He said he was at one of the largest churches in Uganda –a megachurch. Right in the middle of the service, as the preacher was speaking, a seven-year-old boy got out of his seat and walked right down the middle of the aisle toward the front.

The pastor thought that was kind of cute, so he stopped preaching, and the boy came right up to him and said, "May I say something?" The pastor responded by bringing the little boy up on the platform and giving him the microphone. As he did, the boy merely uttered the words, "Jesus is here." As he spoke it, the Spirit of God fell mightily all across that auditorium. Those who were blind could instantly see. Those who were deaf, instantly heard. Those who came on crutches were healed on the spot. I think it was a prophetic picture. God is releasing His authority even to children.

When we hosted the Carlos Annacondia campaign, we saw over a hundred and sixty people get delivered from demonization. It wasn't Carlos who was casting out the demons. Ordinary believers who were on the deliverance team were casting out the demons. As Carlos would pray, demons would manifest. These people were taken to a tent that was pitched next to the auditorium for the sole purpose of ministering to those who were manifesting demons. Then the deliverance team would go to work. Not only were people delivered, but the ministry team was also excited to see how God used them to cast out these demons. God wants to use you to do the same!

ANGELES' MIRACLE

In our church, we had a woman who was not even on the prayer ministry team receive a miracle for herself. Angeles Peart had a terrible herniated disk and was scheduled for surgery. Randy Clark, Tim Storey, and others who carry a strong healing anointing were going to be with us, so she made a decision to postpone the surgery until after the conference. During the conference, I remember making a special effort to have each speaker pray for her, yet there had been no visible results.

On the last day of the conference, at the last session, I remember seeing Angeles sitting in a contorted position. She was weeping because the pain was so excruciating. As her pastor, I felt like telling her to just go home and get the surgery so her pain could be stopped. But I knew the first step was prayer. It's not that I'm against doctors, or don't believe we should heed their counsel. Thank God for their help when that is the vehicle God chooses to bring about healing. But the Word says the *first* thing we should do is pray for ourselves. I have observed that the first thing we will usually do is grab the medicine and then go to the doctor, instead of just obeying. I believe we will see biblical results if we follow the biblical pattern. The Bible says when you are in trouble, you should *first* pray. Every one of us is a priest unto the Lord. We are each members of the priesthood of believers (I Peter 2:5). It's so basic, but we so often miss it.

As Angeles recounted her story, she said that God began to speak to her at this last session of the conference. He told her that she had been looking to men and all of the healing evangelists speakers at the conference, but hadn't really been looking to Him. Then He told her that He wanted to use *her* for her own healing! The Holy Spirit instructed her to lay her own hand on her back. It had never occurred to her to do such a thing. Like most of us, she had been looking for everyone else to pray for her. Now, for the first time, she laid her hand on her own back as the worship continued during the last session.

As she did, she went down under the power of the Holy Spirit! There was no catcher. In fact, I remember seeing her fall in the aisle and thinking to myself how interesting this was since I knew her situation. While she was on the ground resting in the Spirit, she had a vision of the Lord. He was doing surgery on her back. When she got up from the worship time, she was totally and instantly healed of the herniated disk. She went to the doctor again to obtain a documented report. Even though her doctor was an atheist, the final conclusion he drew was that "it was a miracle from God."

As a result of Angeles' healing, her dad and mom came to know the Lord. All of her brothers and sisters have come to know Jesus as well. Who is this woman? She was not even on our ministry team. She is a "nameless and faceless person," yet a believer *with the authority of God.* I believe God raised her up because He wants to anoint His people and let us know we have the authority He gave. As believers, God tells us to lay our hands on the sick and they will recover. Do you believe that *you* have that authority?

♦

CHAPTER TWO

AUTHORITY OF PASTORS

All believers have authority. Of that fact there is no doubt. However, there are important degrees of authority described in Word of God that are reserved for specific purposes and delegated people. Look again at James 5:14: "Is any one of you sick? He should call the elders of the church to pray over him and anoint him with oil in the name of the Lord. And the prayer offered in faith will make the sick person well; the Lord will raise him up. If he has sinned, he will be forgiven."

A SPECIAL AUTHORITY

Please note that this verse instructs us to call elders pastors or (the Bible uses these offices interchangeably) to pray for the sick. The verse does not say to call for teachers or evangelists with a healing anointing, but rather it says call for the elders. Whether or not you have received a particular gift of healing, the Word of God says that if you are a pastor or an elder, He has given you special *authority*. Another confirmation of this authority is found in Hebrews 13:17 where believers are admonished to "obey your leaders and submit to their *authority*. They keep watch over you as men who must give an account. Obey them so that their work will be a joy, not a burden, for that would be of no advantage to you" (italics added). There is another measure of authority given to those to whom God has delegated leadership within His Church. It is delegated by God Himself and carries His endorsement. We can trust in this type of authority and confidently expect God to come through when we call upon it.

Of course, the authority of the pastor and elders is to be used for service, not for abusing those who follow in Christ. But there is no question about it: God has delegated authority to pastors. He has given authority to elders. I believe this also includes those who are in delegated lines of authority in the church from the pastors down. Each of you has also been given authority from God. Just as the Lord delegated authority to His apostles, and to pastors, I believe this same line of authority flows down through leaders of various ministries, such as cell or small group leaders in the church.

We need to tap into that authority, to call upon it, and to believe God for healing and miracles. If you are sick and have first prayed for yourself, but still need results, call for the elders. Call for the pastors. If you need to pursue further, then seek out those with a healing ministry or special gift. Pursue every avenue God has given us for healing. That is using wisdom. Healing is a mystery, and I don't fully understand it, but things happen when we call on those who have been given specific authority by God.

A Curse From China

A couple in our church named David and Connie Debord

adopted a beautiful baby girl from China. When Connie returned from China with her new baby, she became deathly ill with a high fever. She went to the doctors, and they could not determine the nature of the illness. Initially, they believed it to be a severe flu. It lasted for weeks.

She then sought out a specialist in Southern California who made evaluations and informed her that she had a rare form of leukemia. Finally Connie called us and said, "Pastor, I have a

---

WHEN THOSE WHO HAVE THE HIGHEST LEVEL OF
SPIRITUAL AUTHORITY IN A GIVEN CITY TRULY UNITE
AND *START TO EXERCISE THAT AUTHORITY*,
I BELIEVE THAT WE WILL START SEEING CITIES
TAKEN FOR CHRIST.

---

rare leukemia, and they don't know what to do for me." I told her to come to our pastors' prayer meeting held before our service so that we as pastors could pray for her.

She and her husband came to the meeting. As we were praying, one of our pastors, Rick Wright, got a word of knowledge that she had received some kind of curse while she was in China adopting her new daughter. We agreed in prayer together, and began to take authority over that demonic spirit which had attached itself to her in China. That spirit began to manifest, and we continued praying. Within about seven minutes, Connie was set free—totally healed and delivered. She returned for a battery of tests for confirmation, and nothing could be found. Connie has had no more symptoms to this day.

As I witnessed her immediate change and the power of God that was present, I remember thinking, "This is absolutely amazing, Lord. You have given us authority as pastors. When people are sick, when doctors have no solution, we have the authority in the name of Jesus to change things. We have authority to bind and loose."

HOW TO RAISE THE DEAD

The pastors in China understand their authority in Christ. At our last missions conference, one of our guest speakers, Dennis Balcome, shared an interesting and funny story. He was ministering to the pastors of the underground church in China. The Chinese pastors were testifying how the dead were being raised in Jesus' name. Dennis, amazed at the testimonies, asked sincerely, "How do you raise people from the dead?"

There was a stunned silence. These leaders had looked to Dennis as their pastor and were shocked that he would ask such a question. Finally, one of the pastors spoke up, "Why pastor, don't you know? We simply command them to rise from the dead in Jesus' name."

Dennis, realizing that he had asked the wrong question, quickly replied, "Oh I know how to raise the dead, but I was asking you to see if you pastors knew!" Yeah, right. Dennis had never raised anyone from the dead, but these Chinese pastors knew their authority in Christ.

EXERCISING PASTORAL AUTHORITY

God has given us the keys. The Word of God says that whatever we loose will be loosed in heaven. Whatever we bind on earth will be bound in heaven (Matt. 18:18). Pastors, we need to exercise that authority with confidence. We need to train our people to come, seek God, and be prayed over first before they go to the doctor. I'm not saying that pastors should be the only ones praying, but that teams should be raised up under the pastor's authority in every congregation who are able to pray. We can use wisdom and exercise the full limits of the wonderful and powerful authority we have been delegated by God to bring release and healing in His name.

That is why I believe that the highest level of authority in a city are the apostles and pastors. Can you imagine the divine synergy of spiritual authority that can take place when apostles and pastors unite and pray? When those who have the highest level of spiritual authority in a given city truly unite and *start to exercise that authority*, I believe that we will start seeing cities taken for Christ.

Even as I write this, over a hundred apostles, pastors, and intercessors are networking together and praying together under an umbrella organization called CityWatch here in Los Angeles. Our goal is to see a citywide, twenty-four hours of prayer and worship established, as well as to strategically evangelize our city. I believe with the unity and collective authority of these men and woman, we can see revival come to Los Angeles.

CHAPTER THREE

AUTHORITY IN THE NAME OF JESUS

There is incredible power in the name of Jesus Christ. The Word says in James 5:14 that the elders are to "pray over him and anoint him with oil *in the name of the Lord*" (italics added). This is because the name of Jesus represents His full authority. That's why He says that "in My name they will cast out demons; ...and they will lay hands on the sick and they will recover" (NKJ). In Acts 3, when Peter came to the lame man, he knew he had nothing worthwhile of his own to give to the man. Instead, Peter knew he had something far greater. Peter said, "Silver and gold I do not have, but what I do have I give you: *In the name of Jesus Christ of Nazareth,* rise up and walk" (Acts 3:6, NKJ, italics added)!

POWER OF ATTORNEY

When we exercise our authority, we do so in the name of Jesus and on His behalf. You might liken this to the *power of attor-*

ney. The power of attorney means you have been given full permission to act with the full power and authority of another individual. Let me illustrate.

When my family and I first moved to Southern California from Washington, D.C., we were not prepared for the difference in the price of housing. We lived in a house in Washington that was bigger than the house we desired to purchase in Southern California. Yet the smaller house in California was three times more expensive. We simply could not afford to buy it on our own. However, we felt clearly that God had told us to go to the Los Angeles area and establish ourselves because God was going to bring revival. We felt prophetically it was important to buy a house. The only way we could qualify for the property was to have my parents co-own the property with us. Because my parents lived on the east coast, orchestrating all of the necessary paperwork could become quite complicated. To make the transactions easier, my father and mother gave me the power of attorney. In effect, this meant that without them being present, I could use their name to buy the house and transact every legal document needed with their full authority.

The authority in the name of Jesus is the same. The only difference is that He asks you to *exercise faith* in using His name. It's like a double signature check that Jesus has already signed. All you must do now is sign your name under His and use the authority He has already given. Thus, when you cast out demons in His name, it is as if Jesus Himself is casting out the demons. It's the same with raising the dead. When you pray in His name, it is Jesus who is doing the raising. It is God. It's His authority and His power that have been delegated to us, and we are co-laboring with Him. That's why it is called the Great Co-mission. We are laborers with Him, in conjunction with Him.

A PRAYER OF AUTHORITY PRODUCES A MIRACLE

We have His authority to do that which He directs. I'll never forget what happened one Saturday morning, long before the Renewal had begun. I was preparing for the Sunday message, and a church member called me in a panic. She said her mom had just been rushed to the hospital. She was in bad shape, hooked up to a respirator, and the doctors have given her about a month to live. Her lungs had collapsed. My church member was talking about medical things that went way over my head. All I knew was that her mom was in the intensive care unit, and I had to get over there immediately. So I stopped what I was doing and went to the hospital.

When I walked into the intensive care unit, several physicians and nurses were working on the mother. There were tubes and machines hooked up everywhere on her body. You could smell death all over her. As I entered, a physician told me that I could stay and pray as a pastor, but to keep out of the way so the procedures could go on. I put my arm around my church member and began to pray an "evangelistic prayer."

It was the kind of out-loud prayer you pray when you share the gospel so that others in the room can hear it. That's the best I thought I could do at the time, and at least the medical personnel would be exposed to salvation. But God stopped me right in the middle of the prayer and spoke to my heart. He told me He wanted me to take authority over the situation and rebuke the spirit of death. I finished praying my evangelistic prayer – and then began to do what the Lord had spoken. The doctors were listening. I said, "In the name of Jesus, I command the spirit of death to leave this body." When I issued this command, I wish I could say the woman's mother leaped up off the table, pulled out the tubes, and declared she was healed. It didn't happen like that, and it looked as though nothing had changed.

Yet I obeyed and did what the Lord had instructed me to do. The next day, my church member called me and said the doctors didn't know what had happened, but her mother's pulse rate and vital signs were returning to normal. The day after, she reported that her mother was off of the electronic respirator, and that the doctors were amazed she was recovering so quickly. Four days after the prayer, her mother walked out of the hospital. There is great authority in the name of Jesus!

AUTHORITY OVER SUICIDAL DEATH

I remember as a young believer another incident that happened to me. In the mid '70s, when I was about 19 years old, I was invited to a conference by a charismatic Southern Baptist pastor. We had just stopped for lunch and had returned to the Pennsylvania turnpike to finish our drive to Pittsburgh. Suddenly we noticed an accident across the eight-lane freeway.

My elderly pastor friend pulled the car off to the side of the road and asked me to run see if there was anything we could do to help. I ran, making my way through several lanes of traffic, over to the other side. As I got closer to the accident, I saw a person with a flare who was helping out by directing traffic. As I tried to find out what had happened, I learned that a man had apparently pulled his truck over on top of the bridge, and jumped off of the bypass onto the freeway hoping to be hit by a car and commit suicide.

I asked the man with the flare if the person was dead, and he said yes. My heart sank. At that point, I continued toward the accident scene, no longer running, but walking dejectedly. I came upon another person directing traffic and asked again if the person was dead. This man replied that a nurse had just pulled up and examined the man and detected a very, very faint pulse. I hurried toward the man.

As I arrived, there was quite a commotion around this person. The nurse was there, an ambulance had been called, and about seven people were standing around. No one wanted to touch the man. There was blood and body fluids everywhere. No words could accurately describe how the mangled body looked. It was all I could do not to throw up.

I decided to return to my pastor friend and inform him that a nurse was on the scene, an ambulance had been called, and there was nothing more we could do. God stopped me right in

---

GOD WANTS TO USE US LIKE NEVER BEFORE.
HE WANTS TO USE YOU;
HE WANTS TO USE ME.
EXERCISE YOUR AUTHORITY IN HIS NAME!

---

my tracks. He told me to go into the circle of people standing around the man's body, lay my hands on that man, and raise him up in the name of Jesus. My first thought was to rebuke Satan! "No way the enemy is going to make a fool out of me," I thought. "I'm not going in that circle. Heck, I'm just a 19-year-old kid." I started to walk away.

God spoke to me again. "Go into that circle and lay your hands on that man." My heart was pounding a hundred miles an hour; I was breaking out into a cold sweat. I briefly thought about the conference and how miserable I would be if I didn't obey God now. I turned around, approached the circle, and said, "Excuse me." No one knew who I was. I got down on my knees and began to pray very quietly, not touching the body. God interrupted again and said to me, "What are you doing? They don't know what you are doing. You have to pray out loud in My name so that I will get the glory."

I don't remember the exact prayer, though I do remember weaving in the gospel. God once again interrupted me and said, "Enough of your prayer. Pray Mine. Pray in tongues." The onlookers probably thought I was speaking in Korean or something. But I began to pray in tongues, being obedient and believing God. All of a sudden, breath came into the man's body. He regained consciousness, he moved his body, he groaned, and you could hear everyone in the background gasping in awe. He didn't jump up and praise God and leap around, but there was a direct correlation between his regaining consciousness and the prayer. God began to teach me that we have authority in the name of Jesus.

THE LION OF JUDAH: AN OPEN VISION

There are many ways God can confirm to us the authority of His name. One of the most powerful personal encounters I have ever had was an open vision I experienced in 1998. I had been speaking at a healing conference with John Arnott in Toronto. The last night proved to be a miraculous time, and many people were healed. I returned late to my hotel room and went to bed.

I was awakened in the middle of the night by an awful demonic presence in my room. It was a spirit of fear, and suddenly I felt totally paralyzed. This spirit seemed so pervading, so overwhelming, so petrifying, I couldn't even speak. It took all I had to finally utter the name of Jesus. The moment I said the name Jesus, I experienced the second open vision of my lifetime.

I saw an incredible diamond right above me with a huge eyeball looking down. A new, even greater fear came upon me. Yet it was a different kind of fear – it was the fear of the Lord. My spirit catapulted closer to the diamond, and the diamond came closer to me. I saw in detail the eyeball behind the diamond. It was the head of a lion – it was the Lion of Judah. Then the vision shifted from the head of the Lion into a map of the world. Superimposed on the map was a beautiful butterfly. As I observed, the Lord began to speak to me prophetically, saying, "Listen, I am in authority, I am ruling over the nations, and I want to bring salvation to the nations. That butterfly represents salvation." All of a sudden, the demonic spirit was gone.

A Defeated Foe

I was overwhelmed at the magnitude of God and His rule in all the earth. The devil is not in control over the nations or our lives. God is ruling and reigning over the earth. "The earth is the LORD's, and everything in it, the world, and all who live in it" (Psalm 24:1). We are to exercise our spiritual authority to bring the manifestation of His rule to our world. In the midst of demonic onslaught, my heart was being established in the fear of the Lord and His authority. God was teaching me that the name of Jesus invokes that authority. I will never forget it.

When we measure ourselves and our strength, we will not win the battle the enemy wages against us. But when we focus on God's size, His strength, and the breadth of His authority, we will win every time. When Goliath was fighting David, he was comparing himself to David. Because of his superior size and strength, Goliath was confident that there was no competition. In the natural, that appeared to be true. Except in that same battle plan, David was comparing Goliath against *his God*, and there was no contest! The God of David won the battle.

We need to see Satan as he really is – a defeated foe. The story goes that the great reformist Martin Luther had gone to sleep one evening when he felt a demonic presence at the foot of his bed. Apparently, he lit a candle to identify the source, and declared, "Oh, it's only you, Satan." He blew out the candle and went back to sleep. God is saying to each of us as believers, "I am behind you – I am the Lion of Judah, I am ruling and reigning, all authority has been given to Me in Heaven and on earth…therefore…Go and make disciples. Use My name! Exercise My authority!"

A YOUNG'S MAN AUTHORITY

Dale Kaufman, founder of King's Kids International, shares a story about an event that took place during the Lillihammer Olympics. The King's Kids, a division of Youth With a Mission, had been mobilized to evangelize the public during the event. They used every opportunity available to present the gospel during the festivities. The kids were encouraged to be led by the Holy Spirit and share prophetic insights, words of knowledge, and prayer with people they encountered.

One 17-year-old boy walked into a restaurant and heard the Lord tell him to go and sit down next to a certain man. He did so and struck up a conversation. While he was talking to the man, the Holy Spirit began to give him a word of knowledge that the man had a daughter who was dying of cancer. To be sure, he asked the man a few questions. "Are you married?" he inquired. "Yes," came the reply. "Do you have a daughter?" "Yes," the man said. "Does she have cancer?" he asked compassionately.

The moment the boy raised that question, the man broke down and started to weep. "How did you know?" he asked.

The young man then shared the gospel with the man and told him that God cares so much for him that he would tell a stranger about his daughter. He then asked permission to pray for her. The father was sobbing and said, "Of course, please pray."

As soon as he released the boy to pray, the mother and daughter "coincidentally" walked into the restaurant! You could see a cancerous growth protruding from the daughter's neck. In boldness, that 17-year-old boy, who had already received permission from the father, introduced himself to the mother and daughter and quickly explained that the dad had just given him permission to pray. Before he even got a response, he placed his hands on the daughter's neck and rebuked the cancer *in the name of Jesus*. The cancer fell off right there in the restaurant, and a mini-revival broke out on the spot!

The father and mother got down on their knees and began weeping and confessing their sins as fast as they could. People in the restaurant found out what was happening and began turning to God. It was such a commotion that the owner of the restaurant had to call the police to settle the crowd. Who was that 17-year-old boy? A believer who used the authority of the name of Jesus!

I believe that in Jesus' name we are going to start seeing more people raised from the dead. A Hispanic pastor in our city had a woman in his congregation whose baby got a fatal infection when it was born. The church was on a 24-hour prayer alert. The baby technically died twice – showing no vital signs on the monitor. The pastor ran to the hospital and prayed for that child. The baby was raised from the dead. Recently, the baby's mother shared the testimony at a conference at our church. The baby is now a thriving one-year-old!

God wants to use us like never before. He wants to use you; He wants to use me. Exercise your authority in His name!

CHAPTER FOUR

———————◆———————

AUTHORITY IS RELEASED THROUGH FAITH

We release the authority of God through our faith. The Bible says, "and the prayer offered in faith will make the sick person well" (James 5:15). You don't have to wait for a special time or a certain person to anoint you or pray for you personally. Your faith can release your healing and God's authority right now or anytime! Hearing or seeing the testimonies of others is especially helpful in allowing us to release our own faith.

A MIRACLE BY FAITH

Last year, I was in a meeting with Victor Richards, a pastor of a four-thousand-member church in Mexico. It was a pastors' conference, but in the evenings it was opened to the public with about 2,000 people in attendance. The Spirit of God fell, and an atmosphere of faith and healing was released. Many, many people were healed. We called for people to get in line to come forward and tell what God had done for them. Testimony after testimony came forth as people shared about their healing.

Still out in the crowd was a desperate woman who had come to the meeting as a last resort. She had a terminal hydrocephalic condition of water on her brain. She couldn't walk or talk, but she was listening intently to the testimonies. As she heard the words of one girl who was born with crooked feet, and saw her feet now straightened by an instantaneous healing, the hydrocephalic woman was so moved by faith that she just got up out of her chair and began to walk. She was able to stand and talk.

A whole commotion broke out where she had been sitting in the auditorium. I knew something was happening, but I didn't know what. I temporarily stopped the testimonials on the stage and asked what was going on. A pastor shouted back to me, " A woman who couldn't walk or talk is healed." I asked someone to bring her up – and she ran up to me on the stage! She testified the doctors had given her less than four months to live. No one had prayed for her, no one had laid hands on her. She just had faith, and God sovereignly healed her right on the spot! Now she was talking fluently and running around!

FAITH RELEASES AUTHORITY

The prayer offered in faith has power. The act of faith releases God's authority and His power. You simply need to believe it. Yet authority cannot be released without faith – whether you are the Son of God, a pastor, or a believer. Even though we know Jesus had great authority, the Bible says that He could not do many miracles in certain places because of the people's unbelief. When He came to raise Jairus' daughter, He had to clear the room of laughing mockers so that He could create an atmosphere of faith. He then raised her from the dead (Mark 5:40). We must move in an atmosphere of faith to release the full authority of God. We create that atmosphere by preaching the Word, sharing testimonies, intimate worship, and adoration and praise to God which bring the abiding presence of the Holy Spirit.

Over and over again, we find Jesus saying, "Your faith has made you well." His authority was released when it was met with faith. Let me tell you about another such miracle. We have a woman in our church who is now on our pastoral staff. Her name is Brenda. Again this story is in detail and in her own words in my book, *Into The Fire*. She had been diagnosed with multiple sclerosis a number of years ago. She had become debilitated to the point where she couldn't walk without her cane. She could not walk up stairs. Her husband set

---

WE MUST MOVE IN
AN ATMOSPHERE OF FAITH
TO RELEASE
THE FULL AUTHORITY OF GOD.

---

up everything for her downstairs: her bed, her office, everything. One night during a typical renewal service, Brenda heard a testimony about a lady with one blind eye who was healed. She said to the Lord, "It's not fair. Here's a blind person healed. When are You going to heal me?" God then spoke to her and said, "Take off your shoes and run! Do you believe I am here? Take off your shoes and run!"

If you are familiar with M.S., you know that anyone with this condition can barely walk—let alone run—unassisted without falling. Brenda kicked off her shoes and took a few steps. She realized she was instantly healed and began running around our huge auditorium like a woman who was "Holy Spirit possessed!" God healed her in the atmosphere of faith. She took God at His word and saw His authority released. Faith comes by hearing, hearing by the Word of the Lord. Brenda received her miracle by faith!

A Word of Knowledge

Your point of faith for healing may not always come by seeing someone else be healed or by directly hearing the voice of the Lord tell you to "take off your shoes and run," but it may be by a word of knowledge released at a ministry time. Last May in Japan, I was doing a pastor's conference.

A woman from Osaka spent hours on a train coming to the conference. She had breast cancer and cancer of the uterus. I didn't know that and I didn't know her. About 300 people were present at this meeting when I received a word of knowledge about someone fighting cancer. Three people came forward. This young woman was one of them. As she was prayed for, she went down under the power of the Holy Spirit. I had no idea what had happened.

A month later I got a fax from her. When she returned to Osaka and went to the doctors, they could not find any trace of cancer in her body. As a result of her healing, people were hungry for the Living God. It lead to a new church plant including her, her pastor, and a few others, and now the church in Japan is growing.

Her healing not only saved her life, but also spawned a church. So when you hear words of knowledge regarding healing coming forth under the anointing, reach out and receive yours by faith! You can receive healing and life!

START IN FAITH AND STAY IN FAITH

But you have to continue to fight the fight of faith to keep your healing. I have seen people get healed and lose their healing later on. Just like Peter, who stepped out in faith and began to walk on the water, but when he got his eyes off of Jesus and began to look at the circumstances of situation, he began to sink. You have to start in faith and stay in faith.

A woman from San Diego had come to our auditorium to be healed of arthritis. God met her in a wonderful way, and she received total deliverance from the arthritis. A few days later, the symptoms came back. Well she got so mad at the devil. She put her foot down and said, "Devil, I was healed at Harvest Rock Church! I command you to get your hands off of me. I rebuke this spirit of arthritis in Jesus' name!" And the arthritis left, never to return again.

———◆———

CHAPTER FIVE

AUTHORITY IS GIVEN
TO THE RIGHTEOUS

E ven if our faith level is high and we believe we have the full "power of attorney" in Jesus' name, full authority will not be manifest in our lives unless we have corresponding holiness and righteousness.

HOLINESS IS ESSENTIAL TO AUTHORITY

We all have positional righteousness. We are the righteousness of God in Christ Jesus (2 Cor. 5:21). But here I am talking about practicing righteousness. I am talking about walking in holiness. Holiness simply means to be set apart and it has two connotations: to be set apart to God in devotion, love, and intimacy (which is the key to holiness), and to be set apart from sin. Practically, holiness means walking in integrity before Him, having repented of known sin, walking in righteousness and with clean hands before the Lord by His grace and in the power of the Holy Spirit.

James 5:16 says, "The prayer of a righteous man is power-ful and effective." James then goes on to illustrate the word by using Elijah as an example of a righteous man who was given tremendous spiritual authority (vv.17-18): "Elijah was a man just like us. He prayed earnestly that it would not rain, and it did not rain on the land for three and a half years. Again he prayed, and the heavens gave rain, and the earth produced its crops."

I believe that God is saying prophetically that one righteous person can open the heavens of revival by exercising their God-given spiritual authority. Do you believe that? The Bible says that Elijah was "a man just like us," but he was righteous, he had spiritual authority, and God heard his prayers.

It would not make sense for God to bless the authority of someone walking in sin. The Bible declares that sin separates us from God. If we regard sin in our heart, the Lord will not hear (Ps. 66:18). We lose confidence by being cut off. It only follows that it would be hard to rebuke the devil or sickness with any authority if you were not confident you had the back-ing of God.

Sin and Unforgiveness Steal Our Authority

One great inroad of Satan in sickness is his legal access to our bodies when we willfully remain in sin or fail to confess it and gain forgiveness. Psalm 32 describes what happened to David when he hid his sin:

When I kept silent, my bones grew old
Through my groaning all the day long.
For day and night Your hand was heavy upon me;
My vitality was turned into the drought of summer.
I acknowledged my sin to You,

And my iniquity I have not hidden.
I said, "I will confess my transgressions to the
LORD,"
And You forgave the iniquity of my sin.
Psalm 32: 3-5 (NKJ)

I remember a woman who came up to me many years ago
when I was in charge of the healing room at a large weekly
meeting in Washington, D.C. This woman suffered from a
terrible case of arthritis. Her fingers were gnarled and she
could not extend or release them. I prayed for her and nothing happened.

She asked me to pray again, and I did. Nothing happened.
Many times when I pray for people, I do not ask about per-
sonal sin. I sense it is just a time of mercy, a time of prayer.
But I felt strongly that I was to ask her if there was anything

---

I BELIEVE THE ARMY OF MEN AND WOMEN
THAT GOD WANTS TO RAISE UP TODAY
WITH THE SEAL OF HIS SPIRITUAL AUTHORITY ARE
HUMBLE AND BROKEN PEOPLE WHO ARE SUBMITTED
TO A LOCAL CHURCH AND WHO ARE
UNDER PASTORAL AUTHORITY.

---

that was not right in her heart. Like an underground volcano,
she began to spew. She told me that her husband had died
five years previously, and that she had hated him then and
still hated him to that day. She told of his abuse. I assured her
I understood how hard that must have been, but that carrying
this hatred was like poison to her system. He had already
been gone five years and her hatred was as hot as ever! I told

her she had to forgive. She said she couldn't, and that she didn't feel anything. I told her that forgiveness did not have to do with feelings, but rather an act of obedience of a Christian to God's word. I told her about God's immutable law: If you don't forgive, the Father won't forgive you.

After this brief explanation, I asked her how she could withhold forgiveness any longer, and offered to help lead her in a prayer. As I led her in prayer and came to the words, "and I forgive my husband," she began to weep and all the bitterness came out. She was released. We finished the cleansing and forgiveness prayer, and I didn't even have to return to a specific prayer for physical healing. She cried out, "Look, for the first time, I can move my fingers! My arthritis is gone!"

Thus, being willing to repent and forgive is integral to healing, as is receiving forgiveness through the authority which the Lord has given us.

WHEN SOME ARE NOT HEALED

Look again at James 5:15-16. It says the prayer offered in faith will make the sick person well. "The Lord will raise him up. If he has sinned, he will be forgiven. Therefore, confess your sins to each other and pray for each other so that you may be healed. The prayer of a righteous man is powerful and effective."

These verses make two excellent points. Yes, sometimes sin does open the door and give Satan the legal right to attack us. This is not always the case. It is not a simplistic thing. I know some godly people who are fighting physically, and it is not a sin issue. It's a mystery to me why some are not yet healed. One of the best explanations I can give is one taught by Gordon Ladd at Fuller Theological Seminary. He observes, "The Kingdom of God is here, but it is also coming." We have a measure of His kingdom in which we currently walk and enjoy, and yet more of the kingdom and its fullness are also in the process of coming.

AUTHORITY TO FORGIVE

There is also great power and authority released in forgiving one another. Confess your sins to one another. Pray for one another, that you may be healed. There is also something about the authority to forgive sins. Jesus says in John 20:23, "If you forgive anyone his sins, they are forgiven." Do you believe that?

In formal church circles, this is called absolution. I believe this is something that God wants to restore in evangelical and charismatic Christianity. We have authority in Jesus to forgive sins. When people confess, we need to do what the Word says and say, " I forgive you – you are forgiven in Jesus name," and set that person free. Then we will see the release of grace and mercy on that person's life. The Lord has given us that kind of authority.

RECEIVING GREATER AUTHORITY

As we have discovered in this overview of the power authority of the believer, God has given us a great measure of spiritual authority. Through the sacrifice of His Son on the cross, He has gained all authority and allowed us to share in it.

One great key that we must remember, however, is that we operate in godly authority to the extent that God *gives* it to us. We never *take* spiritual authority. We receive it and exercise it within the parameters of the Word of God and His will. Only God can determine how He will give it to you.

I believe that humility is the key of receiving greater authority. The Scriptures make it very clear that you cannot be *in* authority unless you are also *under* authority (Matt. 8: 8-10). The centurion soldier said it well when he said to Jesus, "I, too, am a man under authority."

If you exegete the Scriptures, you will discover by this man's title that he was 3rd in line in authority from the Emperor. Yet he had the wisdom to know the power of properly exercised authority when asking Jesus to heal his servant. He knew that even though Jesus Himself was under authority, the power of the line of authority was so great that Jesus could heal by His word alone! The centurion knew such authority did not even require the physical presence of the Lord for healing, but that His word alone was all-powerful! That is faith and understanding of the power of authority!

Sadly, I know of many believers who grasp for authority and exercise that which has not been given to them. The results are not fruitful and are often destructive. I believe the army of men and women that God wants to raise up today with the seal of His spiritual authority are humble and broken people who are submitted to a local church and who are under pastoral authority. There is mutual accountability and submission.

The days of the lone ranger evangelist or believer are over. It is a corporate time. I believe God wants to pour out more of His Spirit by not only releasing a greater revelation of spiritual authority *to* us, but a greater portion of spiritual authority *upon* us. I would like to conclude this book with prayer that our Father would bring an increase in the revelation and measure of spiritual authority to each one of us.

Matthew 13:12 states that "whoever has will be given more." Ted Haggard from New Life Church in Colorado shared with me a vital principle along these lines. He told me that he believed the key to his church's growth seemed related to spiritual authority, and not his teaching or his programs.

When the church was just getting started, he asked God to give him spiritual authority for a thousand – and He did. With 1,000 in his flock, Ted asked the Lord to give him authority for 2,000. The Lord gave him that measure of spiritual authority. At 2,000, he asked for 5,000. When he reached 5,000 members, he asked God for authority to pastor 10,000 people, and now he's on his way towards 10,000. The point is not the numbers involved, but the principle of the increase of spiritual authority. If you are faithful with little, you shall receive more (Matt. 25: 23).

My exhortation is that you take the authority and faith you already have and use it. Pray for yourself, pray for those the Lord opens to you, and begin to exercise your authority in greater measure. As you do, faithfully and purely, then God shall surely give you more!

PRAYER FOR SPIRITUAL AUTHORITY

I want to lead you in a prayer. If you pray in faith, I believe that you will receive a greater impartation of power and greater spiritual authority. Let's pray.

Father, I come to You in the name of Jesus. Lord, I thank You for Your mercy and Your sacrifice. I thank You that You have given all authority unto Your Son, Jesus, our Savior. I thank You that You have told us to go in that authority and make disciples in all the earth. Lord, I want to be an honorable vessel filled with Your authority. I ask You to search my heart and see if there is any independent spirit or selfish agenda. I repent and take it to the cross. I ask You to show me any way that I am not rightly submitted to the authority You have set in my life. I repent and take that to the cross, too. Lord, I want to be a good servant, found doing what the Master bids, when You return. I desire to see your kingdom come through Your manifest authority.

I am asking You for more, Lord. Take me to the next level, Father. By faith, I will walk in it with grace, humility, and obedience. I ask for more spiritual authority – I am asking for faith and authority to cast out demons, faith and authority to raise the dead, faith and authority to take cities, pull down strongholds, principalities, and powers. Your Word says to ask You for nations, so I ask You to give me nations as my inheritance (Ps. 2:8). Grant me that new measure of authority, Lord, to get the job done and advance Your Kingdom.

I especially ask for authority and impartation in healing. I desire to bring Your release to those who are oppressed – to lay hands on the sick and see them recover for Your glory. These are the signs that follow those who believe in You. I am a believer! (Place your hands on whatever area of your own body that may need healing as you continue to pray.) I have received authority to tread upon serpents and scorpions and over all the power of the enemy. With the authority You have given to me, I rebuke sickness in my body and command the pain to leave. I break every generational curse off my body, every spirit of infirmity, and I loose the healing right now in the name of Jesus. I receive my healing.

I thank you, Lord, that You are now increasing in me the measure of faith and authority to bring this same revelation and release to others. In Jesus' glorious name I pray, amen!

Now, go forth and exercise your faith with authority in Jesus' mighty name!

BIBLIOGRAPHY

Ahn, Ché. *Into the Fire*. Ventura, Calif.: Renew Books, 1998.

Chevreau, Guy. *Catch The Fire*. London, England: Marshall Pickering, 1994.

Annacondia, Carlos. *Listen To Me, Satan*. Orlando, Fla. Creation House, 1998.

For more information on Harvest Rock Church, Harvest International Ministries, and their conferences please call 626-794-1199 or see their website at: www.HarvestRockChurch.org.

Wagner Publications Presents:

RIDDING YOUR HOME OF SPIRITUAL DARKNESS
Chuck D. Pierce & Rebecca Wagner Sytsema

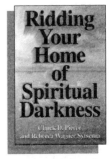

Christians are often completely unaware of how the enemy has gained access to their homes through what they own. This practical, easy-to-read book can be used by any Christian to pray through their home and property in order to close the door to the enemy and experience richer spiritual life. Included are chapters on children, sin, generational curses, and spiritual discernment, as well as a step-by-step guide to praying through your home and a section of questions and answers.
Paperback (75 pp.) • 0.9667481.7.4 • **$7.20 (save 10%)**

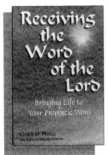

RECEIVING THE WORD OF THE LORD
Chuck D. Pierce & Rebecca Wagner Sytsema

The Bible makes it very clear that God has a plan for our lives. By hearing and receiving the voice of God, we can know our purpose and destiny. In this book you will discover how to hear the voice of God, develop an understanding of prophecy, learn how to test a prophetic word, and experience the joy of responding to God's voice.
Paperback (41 pp.) • 0.9667481.2.3 • **$5.40 (save 10%)**

From C. Peter Wagner . . .

RADICAL HOLINESS FOR RADICAL LIVING
C. Peter Wagner

Can anyone really live a holy life? Is there a test of holiness? *Radical Holiness for Radical Living* answers these and other questions as it opens the way for you to move to new levels in your Christian life. You can defeat Satan's schemes and enjoy daily victory in your walk with God.

Paperback (41 pp.) · 0.9667481.1.5 · **$5.40 (save 10%)**

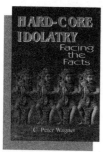

HARD-CORE IDOLATRY: FACING THE FACTS
C. Peter Wagner

This hard-hitting book is destined to clear away the foggy thinking about idolatry that has permeated churches today. This book will help you recognize idolatry (even in some of our churches), confront the schemes of the enemy with more understanding and power, feel the pain of God's broken heart when His people worship idols, and begin to cleanse your home of idolatrous objects.

Paperback (43 pp.) · 0.9667481.4.X · **$5.40 (save 10%)**

REVIVAL! IT CAN TRANSFORM YOUR CITY
C. Peter Wagner

This book answers many questions including: What exactly is revival? Can my city actually be transformed through revival? What steps can be taken to sustain revival in a city? Discover how the Spirit of God can visibly transform our cities through the revival for which we have been praying!

Paperback (63 pp.) · 0.9667481.8.2 · **$5.40 (save 10%)**

How to Cast Out Demons: A Beginner's Guide

Doris M. Wagner

Many modern Christians are now agreeing that we should take Jesus' command to cast out demons more seriously than we have. But how do we do it? Where do we start? This practical, down-to-earth book, written by a respected deliverance practitioner, will show you how.

This one-of-a-kind book will help you to:

- ◆ Take authority over demonic spirits
- ◆ Conduct a private 2-hour prayer appointment
- ◆ Administer a 15-page diagnostic questionnaire
- ◆ Break bondages of rejection, addiction, lust, and more
- ◆ Bring inner healing and break soul ties
- ◆ Set free those whom the enemy has held captive

All this rooted in solid, biblical integrity and done in a calm, safe, controlled ministry environment.

Paperback (201 pp.) • 1.58502.002.8 • **$10.80 (save 10%)**

CONFRONTING THE QUEEN OF HEAVEN

C. Peter Wagner

This book takes a look at what is perhaps one of the most powerful spirits in Satan's hierarchy--the Queen of Heaven. This book answers what we as Christians can do to play a part in confronting the Queen of Heaven and proclaiming that Jesus Christ is Lord.

Paperback (42 pp.) • 0.9667481.3.1 • **$5.40 (save 10%)**

PRAYING THROUGH TURKEY
AN INTERCESSOR'S GUIDE TO AN ANCIENT AND NEEDY LAND
Andrew Jackson
with George Otis, Jr.

This book will take you on a fantastic journey, tracing Christianity from its roots to modern times in the nation of Turkey. Intercessors will receive invaluable instruction on how to pray for the cities and unreached peoples of Turkey.

Paperback (60 pp.) • 1.58502.000.1 • **$5.40 (save 10%)**

Coming soon from Wagner Institute Publishing:

♦ SUPERNATURAL ARCHITECTURE
 by Dr. Stan DeKoven

♦ HOW TO HAVE A DYNAMIC CHURCH PRAYER MINISTRY, *by Jill Griffith*

♦ THE STRATEGIC PRAYER ROOM
 by Chuck D. Pierce & Rebecca Wagner Sytsema

For credit card orders please:
call *toll free* 1-888-563-5150
or fax 1-719-266-8256
or email: Arsenal@cpwagner.net

Or mail order with payment to:
The Arsenal
P.O. Box 62958
Colorado Springs, CO 80962-2958 USA

For bulk orders please:
call: 1-719-277-6776
or email: Wlsales@cpwagner.net

All international orders must be paid by credit card

Name

Street Address
(Cannot deliver to P.O. Box)

Phone

Title	Product Number	Qty.	Total
	Subtotal (carry this amount to other side)		

Order form continued . . .

Shipping Rate Table for US only	Subtotal (from other side)	
Amt. of Subtotal Add		
$50 and under $5		
$50.01-$60.00 $6	CO residents add 6.01% sales tax	
$60.01-$80.00 $8		
$80.01-$100.00 $10		
Over $100.00 10% of order	Shipping (see table)	
For international orders, please call or fax with credit card. Shipping will be calculated for you.	Donation to GHM	
	TOTAL ENCLOSED (US FUNDS ONLY)	

Please allow 10 days for delivery. International orders may require
6 weeks for delivery.

METHOD OF PAYMENT:

☐ Check/Money Order (made payable to The Arsenal)
☐ Credit Card: ☐ **VISA**   ☐ MasterCard   ☐ AMERICAN EXPRESS

Number:_____

Exp. Date:_____ Signature: _____